EMMANUEL JOSEPH

The Leader's Voice, How Public Speaking and Action Transform Relationships and Outcomes

Copyright © 2025 by Emmanuel Joseph

All rights reserved. No part of this publication may be reproduced, stored or transmitted in any form or by any means, electronic, mechanical, photocopying, recording, scanning, or otherwise without written permission from the publisher. It is illegal to copy this book, post it to a website, or distribute it by any other means without permission.

First edition

This book was professionally typeset on Reedsy.
Find out more at reedsy.com

# Contents

| | | |
|---|---|---|
| 1 | Chapter 1: The Power of a Leader's Voice | 1 |
| 2 | Chapter 2: The Art of Storytelling in Leadership | 3 |
| 3 | Chapter 3: Building Trust Through Effective Communication | 5 |
| 4 | Chapter 4: Inspiring Action Through Visionary Leadership | 7 |
| 5 | Chapter 5: The Role of Empathy in Leadership Communication | 9 |
| 6 | Chapter 6: Crafting a Compelling Message | 11 |
| 7 | Chapter 7: The Importance of Nonverbal Communication | 13 |
| 8 | Chapter 8: Overcoming Public Speaking Anxiety | 15 |
| 9 | Chapter 9: The Role of Active Listening in Leadership | 17 |
| 10 | Chapter 10: Leading by Example: Aligning Words and Actions | 19 |
| 11 | Chapter 11: The Impact of Feedback in Leadership | 21 |
| 12 | Chapter 12: Navigating Difficult Conversations with… | 23 |
| 13 | Chapter 13: The Role of Emotional Intelligence in Leadership | 25 |
| 14 | Chapter 14: The Power of Positive Reinforcement | 27 |
| 15 | Chapter 15: Building a Culture of Collaboration | 29 |
| 16 | Chapter 16: The Role of Vision and Mission in Leadership | 31 |
| 17 | Chapter 17: Transforming Relationships and Outcomes Through… | 33 |

# 1

# Chapter 1: The Power of a Leader's Voice

A leader's voice is more than just a means of communication; it's an instrument that can inspire, motivate, and drive change. The power of a leader's voice lies in its ability to convey vision and direction. When leaders articulate their thoughts clearly and passionately, they create a compelling narrative that others can rally around. This narrative becomes a guiding star that illuminates the path forward and aligns the efforts of the entire team.

Effective public speaking is a critical component of a leader's voice. Through public speaking, leaders can address large audiences, share their vision, and galvanize support for their initiatives. The ability to speak confidently and persuasively in public settings amplifies a leader's impact and extends their reach. It's not just about delivering a message; it's about connecting with the audience on an emotional level and making them feel invested in the leader's vision.

Leaders who harness the power of their voice understand the importance of authenticity. Authenticity fosters trust and credibility, which are essential for building strong relationships and achieving long-term success. When leaders speak from the heart and stay true to their values, they create a sense of authenticity that resonates with their audience. This authenticity is the foundation upon which lasting relationships are built.

The power of a leader's voice extends beyond words. It includes actions that back up those words and demonstrate commitment to the stated vision. Actions speak louder than words, and when leaders align their actions with their words, they reinforce their message and build trust. This alignment between words and actions is crucial for transforming relationships and achieving desired outcomes.

# 2

# Chapter 2: The Art of Storytelling in Leadership

Storytelling is a powerful tool that leaders can use to connect with their audience and communicate their vision. Stories have a unique ability to capture attention, evoke emotions, and create memorable experiences. When leaders incorporate storytelling into their communication, they can make their message more relatable and impactful.

Effective storytelling in leadership involves crafting narratives that are relevant to the audience and aligned with the leader's vision. A well-told story can illustrate key principles, highlight successes, and provide valuable lessons. By sharing personal anecdotes and real-life examples, leaders can make abstract concepts tangible and accessible. This not only enhances understanding but also fosters a deeper emotional connection with the audience.

One of the key elements of storytelling is empathy. Leaders who demonstrate empathy in their stories can connect with their audience on a personal level. Empathy allows leaders to acknowledge the experiences and emotions of others, creating a sense of shared understanding. This connection helps to build trust and rapport, making it easier for the audience to embrace the leader's vision and take action.

In addition to empathy, authenticity is crucial in storytelling. When leaders share genuine stories that reflect their true experiences and values, they create a sense of authenticity that resonates with the audience. Authentic stories are more likely to be remembered and acted upon, as they create a strong emotional impact. By being authentic, leaders can inspire and motivate others to follow their lead and contribute to the collective vision.

# 3

# Chapter 3: Building Trust Through Effective Communication

Trust is the cornerstone of any successful relationship, and effective communication is key to building and maintaining trust. Leaders who communicate openly and transparently create an environment of trust and mutual respect. When leaders are honest and forthcoming in their communication, they demonstrate integrity and reliability, which are essential for building trust.

One of the ways leaders can build trust is by being consistent in their communication. Consistency reinforces the message and ensures that the audience receives a clear and unified vision. When leaders consistently communicate their values, goals, and expectations, they create a sense of stability and predictability. This consistency helps to build confidence and trust among team members and stakeholders.

Active listening is another important aspect of building trust through communication. Leaders who actively listen to their audience show that they value their input and perspectives. Active listening involves not only hearing the words but also understanding the underlying emotions and concerns. By actively listening, leaders can address issues, provide support, and build stronger relationships based on mutual trust and respect.

Nonverbal communication also plays a crucial role in building trust.

Leaders' body language, facial expressions, and tone of voice can convey sincerity, empathy, and confidence. Nonverbal cues often speak louder than words and can reinforce the message being communicated. Leaders who are aware of their nonverbal communication and use it effectively can enhance their credibility and build stronger relationships with their audience.

# 4

# Chapter 4: Inspiring Action Through Visionary Leadership

Visionary leadership involves creating and communicating a compelling vision that inspires others to take action. Leaders with a clear and inspiring vision can motivate their team to work towards a common goal and achieve extraordinary outcomes. The key to visionary leadership is the ability to articulate the vision in a way that resonates with the audience and ignites their passion.

An inspiring vision provides a sense of purpose and direction. It helps individuals understand how their efforts contribute to the larger picture and creates a sense of belonging and significance. When leaders communicate their vision effectively, they can align the team's efforts and focus their energy on achieving the desired outcomes. This alignment is essential for maximizing productivity and achieving collective success.

Visionary leaders also understand the importance of setting high expectations and challenging the status quo. By setting ambitious goals and encouraging innovation, leaders can inspire their team to push beyond their limits and achieve remarkable results. This requires a balance between providing support and empowering individuals to take initiative. Visionary leaders create an environment where creativity and risk-taking are encouraged, leading to continuous growth and improvement.

In addition to setting a clear vision, visionary leaders lead by example. They embody the values and behaviors they wish to see in others and demonstrate a commitment to the vision through their actions. Leading by example creates a sense of credibility and authenticity, which inspires others to follow suit. When leaders consistently align their words and actions with their vision, they build trust and inspire others to take action towards achieving the collective goals.

# 5

# Chapter 5: The Role of Empathy in Leadership Communication

Empathy is a critical component of effective leadership communication. Leaders who demonstrate empathy can connect with their audience on a deeper level and build stronger relationships. Empathy involves understanding and acknowledging the emotions and perspectives of others, which creates a sense of shared understanding and trust.

One of the ways leaders can demonstrate empathy is by actively listening to their audience. Active listening involves giving full attention, asking clarifying questions, and reflecting back what has been heard. This shows that the leader values the input and perspectives of others and is willing to engage in meaningful dialogue. Active listening helps to build trust and rapport, which are essential for effective communication and collaboration.

Empathy also involves showing compassion and understanding in response to the needs and concerns of others. Leaders who demonstrate compassion can create a supportive and inclusive environment where individuals feel valued and respected. This fosters a sense of belonging and psychological safety, which are essential for team cohesion and productivity. By showing empathy, leaders can address issues, provide support, and build stronger relationships with their team.

In addition to active listening and compassion, leaders can demonstrate empathy through their nonverbal communication. Nonverbal cues such as facial expressions, body language, and tone of voice can convey empathy and understanding. Leaders who are aware of their nonverbal communication and use it effectively can enhance their connection with the audience and build stronger relationships. Empathy is a powerful tool that can transform relationships and outcomes by fostering trust, collaboration, and mutual respect.

# 6

# Chapter 6: Crafting a Compelling Message

Crafting a compelling message is an essential skill for leaders who want to inspire and influence others. A compelling message is clear, concise, and impactful. It captures the essence of the leader's vision and resonates with the audience. The first step in crafting a compelling message is to define the core message. This involves identifying the key points that the leader wants to convey and organizing them in a logical and coherent manner.

To make the message more engaging, leaders can use storytelling techniques, metaphors, and analogies. These elements add depth and richness to the message, making it more memorable and relatable. Storytelling allows leaders to illustrate their points with real-life examples and personal anecdotes, which can create an emotional connection with the audience. Metaphors and analogies help to simplify complex concepts and make them more accessible.

Another important aspect of crafting a compelling message is considering the audience. Leaders need to understand the needs, interests, and concerns of their audience to tailor their message accordingly. This involves conducting audience analysis and gathering feedback to ensure that the message is relevant and meaningful. By addressing the specific needs and interests of the audience, leaders can create a message that resonates and inspires action.

Finally, a compelling message needs to be delivered with confidence and conviction. The way a leader delivers the message can significantly impact its effectiveness. Leaders need to use appropriate tone, body language, and vocal variety to convey their message with passion and enthusiasm. When leaders speak with confidence and conviction, they create a sense of credibility and authority, which enhances the impact of their message.

# 7

# Chapter 7: The Importance of Nonverbal Communication

Nonverbal communication plays a crucial role in leadership communication. It includes body language, facial expressions, gestures, posture, and tone of voice. Nonverbal cues can convey emotions, attitudes, and intentions, often more powerfully than words. Leaders who are aware of their nonverbal communication and use it effectively can enhance their message and build stronger connections with their audience.

One of the key elements of nonverbal communication is body language. Leaders' body language can convey confidence, openness, and approachability. Positive body language, such as maintaining eye contact, smiling, and using open gestures, can create a sense of trust and rapport with the audience. On the other hand, negative body language, such as crossing arms, avoiding eye contact, or fidgeting, can create barriers and undermine the message.

Facial expressions are another important aspect of nonverbal communication. Leaders' facial expressions can convey a wide range of emotions, from enthusiasm and excitement to concern and empathy. Consistent and genuine facial expressions can reinforce the message and create an emotional connection with the audience. Leaders need to be aware of their facial expressions and use them effectively to enhance their communication.

Tone of voice is also a powerful tool in nonverbal communication. The way a leader speaks, including pitch, volume, and pace, can convey emotions and attitudes. A confident and enthusiastic tone of voice can inspire and motivate the audience, while a monotone or hesitant voice can diminish the impact of the message. Leaders need to use vocal variety to keep the audience engaged and convey their message with passion and conviction.

8

# Chapter 8: Overcoming Public Speaking Anxiety

Public speaking anxiety is a common challenge that many leaders face. It can hinder effective communication and undermine the impact of the message. Overcoming public speaking anxiety involves developing strategies to manage nerves and build confidence. The first step is to prepare thoroughly. Preparation involves researching the topic, organizing the content, and practicing the delivery. The more prepared a leader is, the more confident they will feel.

Another important strategy for overcoming public speaking anxiety is to focus on the audience rather than on oneself. Shifting the focus from self-consciousness to the audience's needs and interests can reduce anxiety and enhance the effectiveness of the communication. Leaders can engage the audience by asking questions, encouraging participation, and using interactive elements. This creates a sense of connection and makes the speaking experience more enjoyable.

Visualization and positive self-talk are also effective techniques for managing public speaking anxiety. Visualization involves imagining a successful speaking experience and envisioning positive outcomes. Positive self-talk involves replacing negative thoughts with positive affirmations. By visualizing success and reinforcing positive beliefs, leaders can boost their confidence and reduce anxiety.

Finally, leaders can use relaxation techniques to manage public speaking anxiety. Deep breathing, mindfulness, and relaxation exercises can help to calm the nerves and reduce physical symptoms of anxiety. Practicing these techniques regularly can build resilience and increase confidence in public speaking situations. By managing public speaking anxiety, leaders can communicate more effectively and inspire their audience.

# 9

# Chapter 9: The Role of Active Listening in Leadership

Active listening is a critical skill for effective leadership communication. It involves fully engaging with the speaker, understanding their message, and responding appropriately. Active listening demonstrates respect and empathy, which are essential for building trust and strong relationships. Leaders who practice active listening can create a positive and collaborative communication environment.

One of the key components of active listening is giving full attention to the speaker. This involves maintaining eye contact, nodding, and providing verbal and nonverbal feedback to show that the leader is engaged. Avoiding distractions and being present in the moment are essential for active listening. By giving full attention, leaders can understand the speaker's message and respond thoughtfully.

Another important aspect of active listening is asking clarifying questions. Clarifying questions help to ensure that the leader understands the speaker's message accurately. They also demonstrate that the leader is genuinely interested in the speaker's perspective. Asking questions such as "Can you explain more about that?" or "What do you mean by that?" can provide valuable insights and deepen the conversation.

Reflecting and summarizing are also key components of active listening.

Reflecting involves paraphrasing the speaker's message to ensure understanding, while summarizing involves providing an overview of the key points. These techniques help to reinforce the message and show that the leader values the speaker's input. By practicing active listening, leaders can build stronger relationships, enhance collaboration, and achieve better outcomes.

# 10

# Chapter 10: Leading by Example: Aligning Words and Actions

Leading by example is a fundamental principle of effective leadership. It involves aligning words and actions to demonstrate commitment and authenticity. When leaders lead by example, they create a sense of credibility and trust that inspires others to follow suit. Leading by example is not just about what leaders say, but also about what they do and how they behave.

One of the ways leaders can lead by example is by embodying the values and behaviors they want to see in others. This involves demonstrating integrity, accountability, and dedication to the vision. When leaders consistently align their actions with their values, they create a sense of authenticity that resonates with their audience. This authenticity fosters trust and credibility, which are essential for building strong relationships and achieving desired outcomes.

Leading by example also involves setting high standards and expectations for oneself. Leaders who hold themselves to high standards inspire others to do the same. This requires a commitment to continuous improvement and a willingness to take responsibility for one's actions. By setting high standards and modeling the desired behaviors, leaders can create a culture of excellence and inspire others to strive for their best.

In addition to setting high standards, leading by example involves recognizing and celebrating the achievements of others. Leaders who acknowledge the contributions and successes of their team members create a positive and motivating environment. This recognition fosters a sense of pride and accomplishment, which can inspire others to continue working towards the collective vision. By leading by example, leaders can create a culture of trust, collaboration, and excellence.

# Chapter 11: The Impact of Feedback in Leadership

Feedback is a powerful tool that can drive continuous improvement and foster growth. In leadership, providing and receiving feedback is essential for personal and professional development. Leaders who effectively give feedback can motivate their team, enhance performance, and build a culture of continuous improvement.

One of the key aspects of giving feedback is being specific and constructive. Specific feedback provides clear guidance on what needs to be improved and how to achieve it. Constructive feedback focuses on behaviors and actions rather than personal attributes, making it more actionable and less likely to be perceived as criticism. By providing specific and constructive feedback, leaders can help their team members grow and develop their skills.

Receiving feedback is equally important for leaders. It requires humility and openness to acknowledge areas for improvement and embrace the opportunity for growth. Leaders who actively seek feedback from their team members demonstrate a commitment to continuous learning and self-improvement. This creates a culture of openness and transparency, where feedback is valued and encouraged.

Creating a feedback-rich environment involves fostering a culture of trust and psychological safety. When team members feel safe to give and receive feedback without fear of retribution, they are more likely to engage in honest and productive conversations. Leaders can promote a feedback-rich environment by leading by example, providing regular feedback, and encouraging open dialogue. By leveraging the power of feedback, leaders can drive continuous improvement and achieve better outcomes.

# 12

# Chapter 12: Navigating Difficult Conversations with Confidence

Difficult conversations are an inevitable part of leadership. Whether it's addressing performance issues, resolving conflicts, or delivering bad news, leaders need to navigate these conversations with confidence and sensitivity. The key to navigating difficult conversations is preparation and a clear communication strategy.

Preparation involves understanding the issue at hand, gathering relevant information, and anticipating potential reactions. By being well-prepared, leaders can approach the conversation with confidence and clarity. It's also important to set a positive and respectful tone at the beginning of the conversation. This helps to create a constructive atmosphere and reduces tension.

During the conversation, leaders need to listen actively and empathetically. Active listening involves giving full attention, acknowledging the other person's perspective, and responding thoughtfully. Empathy involves understanding and validating the emotions of the other person, which helps to build trust and rapport. By demonstrating active listening and empathy, leaders can create a supportive environment where difficult conversations can be resolved constructively.

It's also important to stay focused on the issue and avoid personal attacks or blame. Leaders should address specific behaviors or actions and provide clear guidance on how to move forward. By staying focused and solution-oriented, leaders can navigate difficult conversations with confidence and achieve positive outcomes. Difficult conversations can be challenging, but they are also opportunities for growth and improvement.

# 13

## Chapter 13: The Role of Emotional Intelligence in Leadership

Emotional intelligence (EI) is a critical component of effective leadership. It involves the ability to recognize, understand, and manage one's own emotions, as well as the emotions of others. Leaders with high emotional intelligence can build stronger relationships, navigate social complexities, and make better decisions.

One of the key aspects of emotional intelligence is self-awareness. Self-awareness involves understanding one's own emotions, strengths, and weaknesses. Leaders who are self-aware can manage their emotions effectively and respond appropriately to different situations. This self-awareness also helps leaders to recognize the impact of their emotions on others and adjust their behavior accordingly.

Another important aspect of emotional intelligence is self-regulation. Self-regulation involves managing one's emotions and impulses in a constructive way. Leaders who can regulate their emotions can stay calm and composed under pressure, making them more effective in difficult situations. Self-regulation also involves being adaptable and open to change, which is essential for navigating the complexities of leadership.

Empathy is a crucial component of emotional intelligence. Empathy involves understanding and acknowledging the emotions and perspectives of others. Leaders who demonstrate empathy can build stronger relationships, foster trust, and create a supportive environment. Empathy also helps leaders to address the needs and concerns of their team members, which enhances collaboration and productivity.

Finally, social skills are an important aspect of emotional intelligence. Social skills involve the ability to communicate effectively, build relationships, and manage conflicts. Leaders with strong social skills can navigate social complexities, influence others, and build a positive organizational culture. By leveraging emotional intelligence, leaders can enhance their effectiveness and achieve better outcomes.

# 14

# Chapter 14: The Power of Positive Reinforcement

Positive reinforcement is a powerful tool that leaders can use to motivate and inspire their team. It involves recognizing and rewarding desired behaviors, which encourages individuals to continue performing at a high level. Positive reinforcement creates a positive and motivating environment that fosters growth and productivity.

One of the key aspects of positive reinforcement is recognizing and celebrating achievements. Leaders who acknowledge the contributions and successes of their team members create a sense of pride and accomplishment. This recognition can be in the form of verbal praise, written commendations, or tangible rewards. By celebrating achievements, leaders can boost morale and motivate their team to continue striving for excellence.

Another important aspect of positive reinforcement is providing timely and specific feedback. Timely feedback ensures that the recognition is relevant and meaningful, while specific feedback provides clear guidance on what was done well. By providing timely and specific feedback, leaders can reinforce desired behaviors and encourage continuous improvement.

Positive reinforcement also involves creating opportunities for growth and development. Leaders can provide opportunities for training, mentoring, and career advancement to support the professional growth of their team members. By investing in the development of their team, leaders can create a positive and motivating environment that fosters growth and productivity.

Finally, positive reinforcement requires consistency and fairness. Leaders need to apply positive reinforcement consistently and fairly to ensure that all team members feel valued and appreciated. This consistency and fairness help to build trust and credibility, which are essential for a positive and motivating environment. By leveraging the power of positive reinforcement, leaders can inspire their team to achieve outstanding results.

# 15

# Chapter 15: Building a Culture of Collaboration

Collaboration is essential for achieving success in today's complex and interconnected world. Leaders who build a culture of collaboration can harness the collective strengths of their team and achieve better outcomes. Building a culture of collaboration involves creating an environment where individuals feel valued, respected, and empowered to contribute their ideas and perspectives.

One of the key aspects of building a culture of collaboration is fostering open communication. Open communication involves creating channels for sharing information, ideas, and feedback. Leaders can promote open communication by encouraging team members to speak up, actively listening to their input, and valuing diverse perspectives. By fostering open communication, leaders can create a collaborative environment where ideas can flow freely and innovation can thrive.

Another important aspect of building a culture of collaboration is promoting teamwork. Leaders can promote teamwork by setting clear goals, defining roles and responsibilities, and creating opportunities for team members to work together. Team-building activities and collaborative projects can also help to strengthen relationships and build trust among team members. By promoting teamwork, leaders can create a sense of unity and shared purpose.

Empowerment is also crucial for building a culture of collaboration. Leaders who empower their team members to take initiative and make decisions create a sense of ownership and accountability. Empowerment involves providing the necessary resources, support, and autonomy for individuals to succeed. By empowering their team, leaders can harness the collective strengths and talents of their team members.

Finally, recognizing and celebrating collaborative efforts is essential for building a culture of collaboration. Leaders who acknowledge and reward teamwork and collaboration create a positive and motivating environment. This recognition reinforces the value of collaboration and encourages individuals to continue working together towards common goals. By building a culture of collaboration, leaders can achieve better outcomes and drive collective success.

# 16

# Chapter 16: The Role of Vision and Mission in Leadership

Vision and mission are fundamental elements of effective leadership. A compelling vision provides a clear picture of the future and serves as a guiding star for the organization. A well-defined mission outlines the purpose and values that drive the organization's actions. Together, vision and mission create a sense of direction and purpose that inspires and motivates individuals.

The first step in creating a compelling vision is to articulate a clear and inspiring goal. This involves envisioning a future state that is ambitious yet attainable. A compelling vision should be specific, measurable, and aligned with the organization's values and priorities. By articulating a clear vision, leaders can provide a sense of purpose and direction that aligns the efforts of the entire team.

A well-defined mission outlines the core values and purpose of the organization. It serves as a foundation for decision-making and guides the actions of individuals within the organization. A strong mission statement should be concise, clear, and meaningful. It should reflect the organization's values and priorities and provide a sense of purpose that resonates with the team.

Communicating the vision and mission effectively is essential for gaining buy-in and support. Leaders need to articulate the vision and mission clearly and consistently, ensuring that everyone understands and embraces them. This involves using various communication channels, such as meetings, presentations, and written materials, to convey the vision and mission. By communicating the vision and mission effectively, leaders can inspire and motivate their team to work towards the collective goals.

# 17

# Chapter 17: Transforming Relationships and Outcomes Through Leadership

Transforming relationships and outcomes is the ultimate goal of effective leadership. Leaders who can inspire and influence others can create positive and lasting change. Transforming relationships involves building trust, fostering collaboration, and empowering individuals. Transforming outcomes involves achieving tangible results and driving continuous improvement.

One of the key aspects of transforming relationships is building trust. Trust is the foundation of strong relationships and is essential for effective collaboration. Leaders who demonstrate integrity, authenticity, and empathy can build trust and foster a positive and supportive environment. Trust creates a sense of psychological safety, where individuals feel valued and respected, leading to stronger relationships and better outcomes.

Fostering collaboration is also crucial for transforming relationships. Collaboration involves creating an environment where individuals can work together towards common goals. Leaders can promote collaboration by encouraging open communication, valuing diverse perspectives, and creating opportunities for teamwork. By fostering collaboration, leaders can harness the collective strengths and talents of their team, leading to better outcomes.

Empowerment is another important aspect of transforming relationships and outcomes. Leaders who empower their team members to take initiative and make decisions create a sense of ownership and accountability. Empowerment involves providing the necessary resources, support, and autonomy for individuals to succeed. By empowering their team, leaders can drive continuous improvement and achieve remarkable results.

Finally, transforming outcomes involves setting clear goals, measuring progress, and celebrating successes. Leaders need to articulate clear and ambitious goals that inspire and motivate their team. They also need to establish metrics for measuring progress and hold themselves and their team accountable for achieving the desired outcomes. By celebrating successes and recognizing the contributions of their team, leaders can create a positive and motivating environment that drives continuous improvement and achieves outstanding results.

## The Leader's Voice: How Public Speaking and Action Transform Relationships and Outcomes

**Description:**

In the fast-paced and interconnected world of today, effective leadership hinges on the ability to communicate with clarity and conviction. *The Leader's Voice* dives deep into the transformative power of public speaking and strategic action, unveiling how these elements can shape relationships and drive remarkable outcomes.

This insightful book spans 17 compelling chapters, each meticulously crafted to explore a different facet of leadership communication. From harnessing the art of storytelling to the nuances of nonverbal cues, the book reveals the tools and techniques that leaders can use to connect with their audience on a profound level. It emphasizes the importance of authenticity and empathy, guiding readers on how to build trust and foster collaboration within their teams.

Chapters dedicated to active listening, feedback, and navigating difficult conversations provide practical strategies for leaders to enhance their interpersonal skills. The book also highlights the significance of emotional intelligence and positive reinforcement, empowering leaders to create a motivating and supportive environment.

Through real-life examples and actionable advice, *The Leader's Voice* demonstrates how visionary leadership and consistent alignment of words and actions can inspire and mobilize others. It underscores the crucial role of vision and mission in guiding organizations toward success and shows how leaders can build a culture of collaboration and continuous improvement.

This book is a must-read for aspiring and seasoned leaders alike, offering valuable insights and practical tips to enhance their communication skills and drive meaningful change. Whether you're looking to motivate your team, improve your public speaking, or build stronger relationships, *The Leader's Voice* provides the roadmap to becoming a more effective and impactful leader.

www.ingramcontent.com/pod-product-compliance
Lightning Source LLC
LaVergne TN
LVHW020459080526
838202LV00057B/6042